Happy Days at Playcentre

Written and illustrated
by Nita Yuksel

Published 2024 by
Night Unicorn Books
Auckland, Aotearoa New Zealand
tinyurl.com/nightunicornbooks

A catalogue record for this book is available from the
National Library of New Zealand.

Illustrations painted in watercolour and ink and digitally edited with Krita.

Typeset in Andika

ISBN 978-0-473-71405-5

*For my Mount Wellington Playcentre whānau –
thank you for being my village these past
four years. Love you guys xx*

You joined our Playcentre
as a little one

Took your first steps on
the deck in the sun

Laughing together, we swing high and low

Around the centre
in the wagon we go

Playing with animals,
the puzzle's all done

Making music together
is so much fun!

At kai time we sit
and hear stories read,

then return to our play
content and well-fed

Digging and building,
all covered in sand

A big jump, and
onto the mat we land!

At the carpentry table
we hammer away

Express ourselves
with playdough and clay

Painting on paper,
our hands and
our faces

Riding away to
make-believe places

Gloop on our hands
is a cool sensation

With collage we make
an amazing creation!

Now the time to leave
has come along

But the friendships you've found here will still remain strong

And though we're sad
to see you go,
you'll always be part of
our Playcentre whānau!

www.ingramcontent.com/pod-product-compliance
Lightning Source LLC
Chambersburg PA
CBHW042018090426
42811CB00015B/1679